INSECTS
A to Z

Stephen A. Marshall

FIREFLY BOOKS

A FIREFLY BOOK

Published by Firefly Books Ltd. 2009

Copyright © 2009 Firefly Books Ltd.
Text and photographs copyright © 2009 Stephen A. Marshall
All rights reserved.

No part of this publication may be reproduced, stored in a retrieval system, or transmitted in any form or by any means, electronic, mechanical, photocopying, recording or otherwise, without the prior written permission of the Publisher.

First printing

Publisher Cataloging-in-Publication Data (U.S.)

Marshall, Stephen A.
        Insects a to z / Stephen A. Marshall.
[32] p. : col. photos. ; cm.
ISBN-13: 978-1-55407-555-3 (bound)   ISBN-10: 1-55407-555-6 (bound)
ISBN-13: 978-1-55407-503-4 (pbk.)   ISBN-10: 1-55407-503-3 (pbk.)
1. Insects – Juvenile literature. I. Title.
595.7 dc22   QL467.2M37   2009

Library and Archives Canada Cataloguing in Publication

Marshall, S. A. (Stephen Archer)
        Insects A to Z / Stephen A. Marshall.
ISBN-13: 978-1-55407-555-3 (bound)   ISBN-10: 1-55407-555-6 (bound)
ISBN-13: 978-1-55407-503-4 (pbk.)   ISBN-10: 1-55407-503-3 (pbk.)
        1. Insects—Juvenile literature. 2. Insects—Identification—Juvenile literature. 3. Insects—Pictorial works—Juvenile literature. I. Title.

Published in the United States by
Firefly Books (U.S.) Inc.
P.O. Box 1338, Ellicott Station
Buffalo, New York 14205

Published in Canada by
Firefly Books Ltd.
66 Leek Crescent
Richmond Hill, Ontario L4B 1H1

Cover and interior design by Erin R. Holmes/Soplari Design

Printed in China

The publisher gratefully acknowledges the financial support for our publishing program by the Government of Canada through the Book Publishing Industry Development Program.

Contents

4	INTRODUCTION		19	NET-WINGED MIDGES
6	ARMY ANTS		20	OWLFLIES
7	BUMBLE BEES		21	PAPER WASPS
8	CICADAS		22	QUEEN TERMITES
9	DARNER DRAGONFLIES		23	ROBBER FLIES
10	EARWIGS		24	SPIDER WASPS
11	FIREFLIES		25	TIGER BEETLES
12	GRASSHOPPERS		26	URANIA MOTHS
13	HUMMINGBIRD MOTHS		27	VICEROY BUTTERFLIES
14	ICHNEUMONID WASPS		28	WEEVILS
15	JEWEL BEETLES		29	XYLOCOPID BEES
16	KATYDIDS		30	YUCCA MOTHS
17	LACEWINGS		31	ZEBRA CLUBTAIL
18	MOSQUITOES		32	GLOSSARY

INTRODUCTION

The English language contains about a quarter of a million distinct words, of which around 175,000 appear in the Oxford English Dictionary. That seems like a lot, but it is dwarfed by the millions of different insect species on the planet. This problem of naming all the insects is dealt with by using two Latin or Latinized words to give each species a scientific name. One word (always capitalized) refers to the genus, which is a group of related species. The second word (never capitalized) is the species name. The resultant unique names are always written in italics. For example, *Musca domestica* is the common House Fly. About a million insects have been given these sorts of formal names so far, so it would be easy to pick from all those names to find 26 insects with scientific names fitting the 26 letters of the alphabet, but most readers would probably be put off by unpronounceable names like the flies *Prolasioptera aeschynanthusperottetii* and *Parastratiosphecomyia stratiosphecomyoides* and prefer names like Honey Bee, army ant and tree cricket.

The 26 entries in this book are almost all drawn from English words rather than the formal scientific names of insects. Those English combinations, however, require a bit of explanation. First of all, common names differ from time to time and place to place. Thus, the sand fly of South America, the sand fly of North America, and the sand fly of New Zealand are not the same thing (they are in the three different families Psychodidae, Ceratopogonidae and Simuliidae). Just as the same common name can be applied to more than one species, well-known species often have many different "correct" common names. For example, the Corn Earworm, Tomato Fruitworm and Cotton Bollworm are caterpillars of the same species of moth (with the unique scientific name *Helicoverpa zea*).

Good common names are memorable and tell us a lot about the habits, habitats or appearance of the species they describe, and they also usually adhere to a few useful conventions. When you see a capitalized common name (House Fly) it means that it is a proper name for a single species, but if it is in lower case (grasshopper) it refers to more than one species. If a common name includes an order name like "fly" as a separate word it means that the insect really is a fly (a member of the order Diptera), whereas if the order name is part of a compound word it just means that there is a superficial or imaginary similarity. A House Fly is indeed a fly, a dragonfly is not a fly but it would be pretty cool to see a dragon fly. Have fun!

ACKNOWLEDGMENTS

With a million or so insect names available to choose from, picking the right scientific name to go with a specimen or photograph often requires the help of an expert taxonomist who has specialized knowledge of a particular group of insects. To make sure that the names in this book are as accurate as possible I consulted with various other specialists, including Allen Sanborne, Andrew Bennett, Chuck Bellamy, Greg Courtney, Eric Fisher, Robert Anderson, Marc Branham, Sheila Colla, Joshua Jones and John Oswald; they are gratefully acknowledged for their generous help.

DEDICATION

This book is dedicated to my sons, Alexander and Stephen, both great field companions and accomplished bug-spotters.

ARMY ANTS		
EXAMPLE SPECIES		*Eciton burchellii*
DIET		Insects and other small prey
PHOTOGRAPHED		Costa Rica
SIZE		Under half an inch

Army ants are among the most amazing ants, and an advancing mass of army ants is an awesome sight as swarms of workers, guarded by fearsomely big-jawed soldiers, spill over the forest floor in search of prey. Individual army ants are blind and relatively harmless, but the tens of thousands of ants that form the fan-shaped front of an army ant raid can flush out and kill almost all arthropods along their path. They may also kill some vulnerable vertebrates, like little lizards or small snakes, but other insects and related invertebrates make up most of their harvest. Army ant colonies are nomadic, staying put while the queen lays enormous numbers of eggs (sometimes tens of thousands in a week or so), but moving on when the growing colony outstrips the local food supply. This is *Eciton burchellii,* an abundant Central and South American army ant species.

BUMBLE BEES

EXAMPLE SPECIES	*Bombus impatiens*
DIET	Pollen
PHOTOGRAPHED	Canada
SIZE	Half an inch

Bombus transversalis
from Bolivia

Bumble bees bombard pollen by buzzing loudly while visiting flowers. Buzzing helps break pollen free from a flower's anthers, allowing bumble bees to extract pollen from some kinds of flowers hundreds of times faster than honey bees and other bees can. Many cultivated plants, like tomatoes and peppers, are normally "buzz pollinated." Bumble bees are social bees that usually nest underground in hidden places, like abandoned mouse nests, where the queen lays the eggs and stays in the nest while workers search for pollen. These bulky, fuzzy bees are generally found at cooler latitudes and altitudes, and they are most common in temperate regions. This male bumble bee visiting an Impatiens (Jewelweed) flower looks, appropriately enough, like *Bombus impatiens*, a very common eastern North American bee now widely used for pollination in greenhouses.

7

Tettigades from Chile

CICADAS

EXAMPLE SPECIES	*Quesada gigas*
DIET	Tree sap
PHOTOGRAPHED	Costa Rica
SIZE	Length about 1.5 inches

Cicadas, like this newly emerged Costa Rican adult clinging to a cut twig beside its cast nymphal skin, can congregate in impressive numbers when they emerge to suck sap from twigs and branches of trees. Most of the cicada's life is spent underground as a wingless nymph that sucks sap from tree roots, with adults only appearing for a few days. Adult males make their active above-ground days noisy ones, creating a cacophonous buzz by rapidly wobbling a drum skin-like structure at the base of the abdomen.

DARNER DRAGONFLIES

EXAMPLE SPECIES	*Anax junius*
DIET	Other insects
PHOTOGRAPHED	Canada
SIZE	Three inches long

A newly emerged Green Darner and its cast nymphal skin (exuvium).

Darner dragonflies used to be called "devil's darning needles" because of stories about diabolical dragonflies dashing down from the skies to sew up the lips of liars. Dragonfly adults scoop up adult mosquitoes and other small flying insects in a spiky basket made using their six bristly legs, and then chomp down on their prey with massive mandibles. Their young stages (nymphs) live in the water, where they capture mosquito larvae and other aquatic organisms by swiftly shooting out an extensible lower lip. The female of this pair of adult Green Darners (*Anax junius*) is inserting eggs in aquatic vegetation while her mate uses claspers at the tip of his abdomen to guard her by holding on right behind her head.

E arwigs, like this European Earwig (*Forficula auricularia*) are excellent parents as insects go, guarding their eggs from enemies and continuing to tend their small nymphs after the eggs have hatched. Their pincer-like tails can be used to hold enemies or prey, and many earwigs can also squirt their foes with sprays of nasty chemicals from glands near the front of the abdomen. The European Earwig is a common pest accidentally introduced (on multiple occasions) from Europe to North America, where it is now a common nocturnal insect known to eat all sorts of things from flowers to other insects. Earwigs make up the entire order Dermaptera, named for the short skin-like front wings that usually conceal intricately folded hind wings. Most of the world's 2000 or so species of earwigs occur in the tropics.

EARWIGS

EXAMPLE SPECIES	*Forficula auricularia*
DIET	Almost anything organic
PHOTOGRAPHED	Canada
SIZE	Three quarters of an inch

Labia minor, the Lesser Earwig

FIREFLIES	
EXAMPLE SPECIES	*Photinus,* unidentified species
DIET	Small invertebrates
PHOTOGRAPHED	Costa Rica
SIZE	Half an inch

Fireflies perform the fantastic feat of flying while apparently on fire, with a faux flame that "burns" by a chemical reaction that produces light but almost no heat. The resultant familiar firefly flashes serve both to attract mates and to warn potential predators away, since these common beetles are usually loaded with bad-tasting or even poisonous chemicals. Some fireflies fake the flash pattern of other species, luring them to their deaths. Females of some relatively large fireflies (*Photuris* species) deliberately attract the relatively small males of another genus (*Photinus*) with a flash that fools those unlucky males into thinking they are homing in on a waiting female of their own species. The larger females eat the *Photinus* males, stealing their valuable defensive chemicals for their own use.

Unidentified *Photuris* species from Costa Rica.

GRASSHOPPERS

EXAMPLE SPECIES	*Eumastax,* unidentified species of monkey grasshopper
DIET	Foliage
PHOTOGRAPHED	Bolivia
SIZE	Just over an inch

Unidentified Bolivian grasshopper

Grasshoppers generally feed by using massive mandibles to grind green plants. Globally, the worst pests in this group are gregarious grasshoppers called locusts that grow extra-long wings and form gigantic migratory groups (swarms) only when they grow up under crowded conditions. The term "grasshopper" refers to several different families that are grouped together because they have huge hind legs for jumping and short antennae. Some of the strangest-looking grasshoppers are in the tropical family Eumastacidae (monkey grasshoppers or airplane grasshoppers). Grasshoppers in this group, which have unusually narrow wings that leave much of the abdomen exposed, abound in weedy areas along forest edges in Central and South America.

H Hummingbird moths (*Hemaris* species) hover over flowers on hot summer days, looking and sounding much like their hummingbird namesakes. This Hummingbird Clearwing (*Hemaris thysbe*) is uncoiling its long proboscis into some Joe-Pye weed blossoms. Its hovering body is almost motionless above the flowers. Hummingbird moths belong to the sphinx moth family (Sphingidae), a group of stout-bodied, long-winged moths also known as hornworms because of the prominent tail, or horn, on the fat caterpillars in this family. Only a few moths in this family fly during the day, while most seek pale, nectar-filled flowers during the evening or night. Some Sphingidae have a tremendously long proboscis and are specialized pollinators of one or a few kinds of long-necked flowers.

HUMMINGBIRD MOTHS	
EXAMPLE SPECIES	*Hemaris thysbe*
DIET	Nectar. Larvae eat leaves of honeysuckle and hawthorne
PHOTOGRAPHED	Canada
SIZE	Wingspan around two inches

EXAMPLE SPECIES	*Dolichomitus irritator*
DIET	Insect larvae that bore in wood.
PHOTOGRAPHED	United States
SIZE	Just over an inch, without ovipositor

I Ichneumonid wasps are incredibly diverse parasitoids that inject eggs into, or onto, invertebrate hosts including other insects, invariably resulting in the death of the host as the wasp's larva grows. The ichneumonid wasps (family Ichneumonidae) make up one of the largest families of living things, and include many beneficial species that kill insect pests that harm crops and forests. This female wasp is drilling into a fallen tree, and will squeeze an egg down her egg-laying tube (ovipositor) into the tree, where it will pop out and onto a host insect larva (probably a wood-boring beetle). The Ichneumonidae plus the closely related and similar parasitoid family Braconidae together probably include over 100,000 species.

J Jewel beetles belong to the family Buprestidae, for which the common names "jewel beetles" and "metallic wood-boring beetles" are justified by the adult beetles' gem-like wing covers and the juvenile beetles' wood-boring habits (the larvae are also called flat-headed wood-borers). Some jewel beetle species are serious pests that jeopardize the health of whole populations of valuable trees. The Emerald Ash Borer, for example, is an Asian jewel beetle species accidentally introduced to North America where it is killing native ash trees. Despite the few pest species, most beetles in the family Buprestidae are harmless living gems, resplendent in metallic colors that shimmer and shine as the physical structure of their iron-hard cuticle reflects light in special ways. Jewel beetles are found world-wide.

A small *Anthaxia* jewel beetle on a flower in Chile.

JEWEL BEETLES

EXAMPLE SPECIES	*Dactylozodes conjuncta*
DIET	Adults eat pollen, larvae bore in trees
PHOTOGRAPHED	Chile
SIZE	One inch

Katydids and their relatives (Tettigoniidae) listen keenly with their knees, using ear-like structures on their legs, to hear the songs produced by potential mates. The songs, produced by rubbing a scraper on one wing against a file on the other, serve to bring males and females together. Once they meet, the male can give the female a packet of sperm, which is attached to a nutritious jellylike bag (called a spermatophylax) that stays outside the female's body until she eats it. This pair of dead leaf-mimicking katydids includes a relatively large female with a prominent sword-like egg-laying tube (ovipositor), and a smaller male, both with front wings (tegmina) that look remarkably like dead leaves. Look closely at the base of the female's ovipositor to see a glistening white spermatophylax.

KATYDIDS

EXAMPLE SPECIES	*Mimetica mortuifolia*
DIET	Foliage
PHOTOGRAPHED	Costa Rica
SIZE	About two inches

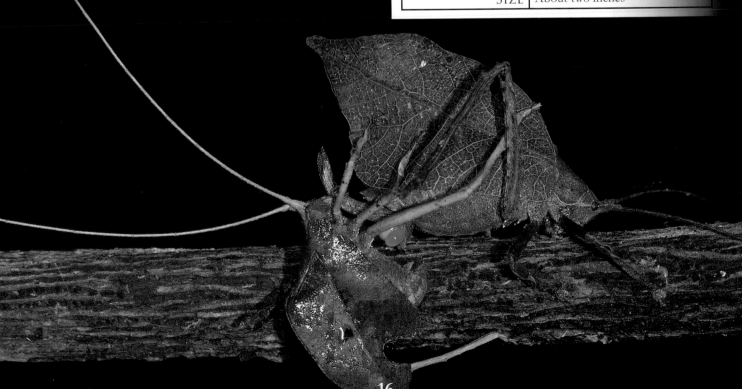

L Lacewings are most likely to be located low among leaves and other greenery where they look for aphids and the other small insects on which both adult and larval lacewings feed. Green lacewings, like this one, lay their eggs at the ends of long stalks so the newly hatched larvae are less likely to be eaten by their hungry brothers and sisters. Green lacewings are often attracted to lights at night, where some species are particularly striking for their glowing golden eyes, and some species are distinctive for their strong musky smells. Look closely at this Goldeneye Lacewing (*Chrysopa oculata*) for a little biting midge piercing its wing veins and feeding on the "blood" (haemolymph) within. Green lacewings and brown lacewings join antlions, mantisflies, spongilla flies, owlflies and a few other uncommon families of insects to make up the order Neuroptera (nerve-winged insects), a group that gets its name for the many veins ("nerves") in the wings.

LACEWINGS

EXAMPLE SPECIES	*Chrysopa oculata*
DIET	Aphid and other insects
PHOTOGRAPHED	Canada
SIZE	About an inch in length

M osquitoes molest us with mouthparts made of multiple blades (mandibles and maxillae) that surround a middle needle-like part that injects us with itch-inducing anticoagulants. Male mosquitoes don't bite, but the bites of their bloodthirsty mates sometimes transmit microorganisms that cause a myriad of maladies. Malaria is the most serious mosquito-borne disease and may be the most significant of all diseases that afflict humankind. Malaria is caused by malevolent microbes (protists in the genus *Plasmodiuim*) that kill hundreds of thousands of people every year, mostly in tropical countries. This blood-filled mosquito sitting on a window screen belongs to the only genus that transmits malaria, the genus *Anopheles* (although this particular species does not normally transmit malaria). Mosquito larvae are aquatic, feeding by filtering microscopic organisms out of calm waters or (like *Anopheles* larvae) from the surface of calm waters.

MOSQUITOES

EXAMPLE SPECIES	*Anopheles naevai*
DIET	Adult females suck vertebrate blood; aquatic larvae feed on surface film
PHOTOGRAPHED	Costa Rica
SIZE	Body length about half an inch

Anopheles quadrimaculatus photographed in Ontario.

NET-WINGED MIDGES

EXAMPLE SPECIES	*Blepharicera,* unidentified species
DIET	Adult males don't eat, females eat other insects. Larvae scrape food from rocks in rushing rivers.
PHOTOGRAPHED	United States
SIZE	Body length less than an inch.

Net-winged midges, named for the networks of narrow creases on their wings, normally live near swift streams and rivers in which their flattened larvae use hydraulic suckers (like suction cups on the underside of the body, six per larva) to cling to even the slickest of water-whipped rocks. Adults of many species, including most members of this genus (*Blepharicera*), use their long legs to hang under the leaves of riverside vegetation in a characteristic pose. Males, like this one, don't seem to do much other than seek mates and perhaps sample a bit of nectar, but females of some species are predators that hunt and kill other insects.

Net-winged midge *Edwardsina* sp larvae from Chile.

19

Owlflies are powerful predators that make up one of only a few families in the odd little order Neuroptera, or "nerve-winged insects." Other Neuroptera, such as antlions and lacewings, are also predators, but owlflies are stronger fliers with conspicuously bigger eyes than other insects in the order. This owlfly is clinging under a twig in a characteristic rest position. Once it opens its wings and takes flight it will become almost dragonfly-like in speed and maneuverability. Owlfly larvae are also predators. Instead of chasing down prey in flight, however, they conceal themselves under bark or in leaf litter. From here they ambush their prey using long, sickle-shaped, hollow mandibles. Members of the owlfly family (Ascalaphidae) occur worldwide.

	OWLFLIES
EXAMPLE SPECIES	*Ululodes*, unidentified species
DIET	Other insects
PHOTOGRAPHED	Bolivia
SIZE	Length about two inches

P Paper wasps pulverize wood pulp to prepare paper nests where they provide their progeny with pre-chewed invertebrate prey. Many species, like this originally European species (*Polistes dominula*), have spread out from their natural ranges, often with our accidental help. As a result, their hunting activities can have devastating affects on local insect populations. A single egg is laid in each nest cell by one or more queens. Worker females harvest a wide variety of other arthropods, sometimes including rare or endangered native insects, to feed the developing larvae. The colony in this photograph is in a sun-blasted rock wall in central Chile. The worker wasp in the foreground is acting like a living fan to cool the colony down.

EXAMPLE SPECIES	*Polistes dominula*
DIET	Other insects
PHOTOGRAPHED	Chile
SIZE	One inch

Polistes instabilis larvae in the nest and adults on the nest, shot in Costa Rica.

QUEEN TERMITES

EXAMPLE SPECIES	*Nasutitermes,* unidentified species
DIET	Wood
PHOTOGRAPHED	Bolivia
SIZE	Two inches

A new queen before taking her mating flight, shedding her wings, and starting a new colony.

Queen termites are quintessential egg-laying machines that produce thousands of eggs. That adds up to millions of progeny before the queen calls it quits at an impressively old (for insects) age that may exceed 15 years. The queue of pale workers and querulous soldiers attending this obese queen includes both males and females (in contrast with the all-female labor forces found in colonies of social wasps and ants). The pointy-headed soldiers of this kind of termite are nicknamed "nailheads" because of their nozzle-like noses, which are used to squirt caustic glue onto attacking ants and other enemies. Termites eat wood or other high-cellulose food that they digest with the aid of helpful microorganisms.

R obber flies are rapacious insects that regularly impale a range of other invertebrates, running them through with sword-like beaks and injecting them with saliva containing nerve poisons and enzymes that dissolve the victims' body contents. The robber fly's face and eyes are protected by a distinctive tuft of hairs, called a mystax, just above the forward-facing beak that characterizes this group of flies. This Costa Rican robber fly (a member of the widespread genus *Ommatius*) is drinking the liquefied body contents of its unfortunate prey (itself an interesting fly called a "micropezid"). The robber fly family (Asilidae) is a large one, including tiny species inclined to attack springtails and midges, as well as massive species able to take down dragonflies and bumblebees.

Pilica formidolosa from Costa Rica.

ROBBER FLIES	
EXAMPLE SPECIES	*Ommatius,* unidentified species
DIET	Other insects
PHOTOGRAPHED	Costa Rica
SIZE	Just under an inch

Spider wasps sting and subdue spiders, which they drag back to their nests to serve as sustenance for their developing larvae. Some spider wasps, such as this shimmering silvery-gold Central American species in the specialized genus *Auplopus*, strip their spider prey of legs before starting the trip back to their nest. An egg is laid on the paralyzed spider in the nest. Spider wasp nests are usually simple burrows in which paralyzed spiders survive immobile until partially eaten by the wasp's larva. Most spider wasps are docile insects that rarely sting in self-defense but some, especially those that hunt huge spiders like tarantulas, are strikingly well-armed with stings you would be wise to avoid. Spider wasps make up a large family (Pompilidae) related to yellowjacket wasps and ants.

Auplopus mellipes from Canada, with its legless, paralyzed spider prey.

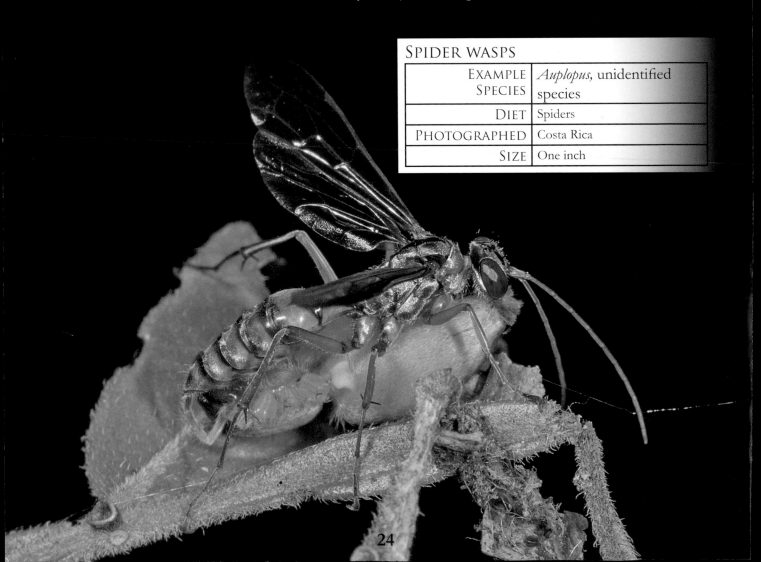

SPIDER WASPS	
EXAMPLE SPECIES	*Auplopus*, unidentified species
DIET	Spiders
PHOTOGRAPHED	Costa Rica
SIZE	One inch

TIGER BEETLES

EXAMPLE SPECIES	*Megacephala,* unidentified species
DIET	Mole crickets and other insects
PHOTOGRAPHED	Bolivia
SIZE	About three quarters of an inch

A North American tiger beetle (*Cicindela* sp) larva pulled from its burrow.

Tiger beetles, like these two tropical beetles, are toothy predators that use their big eyes to seek other insects to tear apart and mash to a pulp using enormous three-toothed mandibles. Brilliantly metallic tiger beetles are often seen standing in the sunshine as they search for insect prey, but the big-eyed members of the genus shown here (*Megacephala*, the big-headed tiger beetles) hunt at night. Big-headed tiger beetles often hunt underground prey such as mole crickets, detecting them by sound more than sight. The male of this pair is not biting his mate, but guarding her from other males. Temperate tiger beetles are most often seen seeking prey in the sunshine of beaches and other exposed patches of ground, but many tropical species use tree leaves as platforms from which to launch attacks on passing prey.

The Sunset Moth of Madagascar (*Chrysiridia riphaeus*) is closely related to the South American Urania moths, and even feeds on the same genus of plant (*Omphalea*).

U

Urania moths are unmistakable insects with ultra-bright iridescent wing bands and unusual tails like those of a swallowtail butterfly. These tropical moths usually live near their host plants (certain kinds of vines), but some undertake unique seasonal migrations every few years. *Urania* species are often seen on the banks of rivers in Central and South America as they seek needed salts on wet mud or soil. Unlike most moths, Urania moths are active during the day, and are often seen feeding at flowers. The four species of *Urania* are neotropical (mostly South and Central America, ranging north to Texas) but other members of the family Uraniidae occur throughout the tropics.

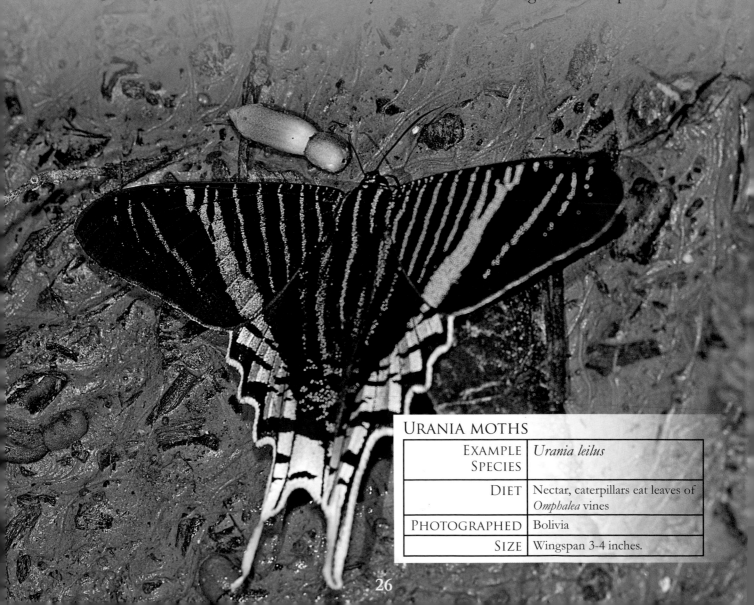

URANIA MOTHS

EXAMPLE SPECIES	*Urania leilus*
DIET	Nectar, caterpillars eat leaves of *Omphalea* vines
PHOTOGRAPHED	Bolivia
SIZE	Wingspan 3-4 inches.

VICEROY BUTTERFLY

EXAMPLE SPECIES	*Limenitis archippus*
DIET	Adult butterflies take nectar; larvae eat foliage of willow and other plants
PHOTOGRAPHED	Canada
SIZE	Wingspan around 3 inches

Viceroy Butterflies (*Limenitis archippus*) are often viewed as vulnerable insects that dissuade birds from eating them through a visual similarity to Monarch Butterflies, which are foul-tasting or even poisonous due to their milkweed diet. In fact, Viceroys eat a variety of vegetation, sometimes sequestering chemicals that render them distasteful, and sometimes not. So Viceroys can either be vulnerable butterflies mimicking a truly toxic species, or they can be chemically protected butterflies with their bright orange colors sending a valid warning message to potential predators.

27

Weevils

Example Species	*Lixus,* unidentified species
Diet	Plants
Photographed	Costa Rica
Size	Half an inch

Chilean *Ryephenes* weevil.

Weevils are the most widely recognized beetles with well-defined snouts. They could well comprise the world's most wildly diverse animal group with about 10 times as many species as there are bird species. Most species develop as legless grubs hidden away inside stems, seeds or other organic material, sometimes doing serious damage to important crops like cotton. The one in this picture is a Costa Rican species in the genus Lixus, a large and distinctive genus of fuzzy weevils. Like all weevils, this adult weevil has chewing mandibles at the end of its distinctive snout.

X

Xylocopid bees (family Xylocopidae) are extra-big bees that make their nests in solid wood, earning a scientific name with the "xylo" prefix as well as the more familiar name "carpenter bees." Some other families of insects that live in wood, for example xylomyid flies and xylophagid flies, have scientific names beginning with the same prefix. Female xylocopid bees, which usually look like large black bumblebees, stock their nests with pollen that serves as food for the bee's larva. Unlike the related bumble bees and honey bees, but like most other bees, xylocopid bees are not social and do not form colonies, although several bees may make their nest burrows close together. This is a male *Xylocopa micans* from the southeastern United States.

Bolivian carpenter bee.

XYLOCOPID BEES

EXAMPLE SPECIES	*Xylocopa micans*
DIET	Pollen
PHOTOGRAPHED	United States
SIZE	1 inch

Y ucca moths are always associated with the yellowish white flowers of yucca plants. Yucca flowers are entirely dependent on yucca moths to transfer pollen from plant to plant and yucca moths are, in turn, entirely dependent on yucca flowers in which their caterpillars develop. However, not all yucca moth species are good pollinators. One species is even known as the "Bogus Yucca Moth" because it does not pollinate its host flowers. This *Tegeticula yuccasella*, photographed in an eastern Canadian garden, is one of the yucca moth species that places pollen on the stigma of its host flower after laying eggs in the flower's ovary. Yucca plants are widely planted in European gardens but they will not set seeds because yucca moths do not yet occur in Europe.

YUCCA MOTHS

EXAMPLE SPECIES	*Tegeticula yuccasella*
DIET	Yucca flowers
PHOTOGRAPHED	Canada
SIZE	Wingspan almost one inch

Z Zebra Clubtails are denizens of swift, clean rivers and streams in which they lay eggs by zig-zagging along the water surface, zipping along in an erratic fashion and periodically dipping the abdomen into the water to deposit an egg. The eggs hatch into predacious nymphs that develop in sandy-bottomed zones with relatively lazy currents. The squat nymphs hide horizontally in the sand, and grab passing prey (such as other aquatic insects, tadpoles or small fish) using an extensible, hinged lower lip. Once fully grown (at about two years old) the nymphs clamber onto the shore to transform into zebra-striped adults that feed on small flying insects. Zebra Clubtails belong to a group of dragonflies called clubtails (family Gomphidae) because of the club-like swollen tip of the abdomen. Many clubtails are rare and getting rarer as the clean streams they prefer become polluted, and Zebra Clubtails are listed as endangered species in some states. Look for them perching horizontally on streamside leaves.

Clubtail dragonfly nymph.

ZEBRA CLUBTAIL

EXAMPLE SPECIES	*Stylurus scudderi*
DIET	Other aquatic invertebrates and small fish
PHOTOGRAPHED	Canada
SIZE	2 inches

GLOSSARY

Abdomen – the third part of the insect body, behind the thorax. Insects are divided into three main parts, the head (with eyes, antennae and mouthparts), the thorax (with legs and usually wings), and the abdomen (which usually has no visible appendages).

Altitude - height or elevation (as you go up a mountain the altitude gets higher).

Anthers – the part of a flower that produces pollen, held up on a stalk called a stamen.

Anticoagulants – something that prevents blood from clotting.

Arthropods – invertebrates with jointed legs. Spiders, shrimp, lobsters and insects are arthropods.

Bioluminescent – light produced by a living organism.

Colonies – groups of related individuals living together, especially groups of social insects.

Family – a group of related genera. All living things are grouped into classes (like the Insecta), orders (like Lepidoptera, the butterfly and moth order), families (like Culicidae, the mosquito family), genera, and species. Family names all end in "–idae".

Genus – a group of closely related species. For example, the House Fly (*Musca domestica*) is one of several species in the genus *Musca*. Genus and species names are always given in *italics*.

Gregarious – animals that prefer to be with crowds of their own kind.

Host – an organism on which, or in which, another organism lives.

Invertebrate – a spineless animal, such as an insect or worm.

Juvenile – young stage of an animal.

Larva – the young stage of an insect with complete metamorphosis, like a caterpillar or grub. Larvae have no visible wing buds.

Latitude – position north or south of the equator. High latitudes are far from the equator.

Mandibles – the insect's jaws.

Metamorphosis – the change from an immature form to an adult form

Migratory – animals that make mass seasonal movements, like Monarch Butterflies or most songbirds.

Neotropical – the New World tropics (Central and South America).

Nocturnal – active at night.

Nomadic – without a fixed place to live, regularly moving from place to place.

Nymph – the young stage of an insect with incomplete metamorphosis, with external wing buds.

Organism – any living thing, such as an animal, plant, fungus or insect.

Ovary – egg chamber in animals or seed chamber in plants.

Ovipositor – egg-laying tube.

Parasitic – living on a single host.

Parasitoid – an organism that lives on, or in, a single host and ultimately kills it.

Pollinators – insects or other animals that transfer pollen from flower to flower.

Predator – an animal that preys on other animals for food.

Proboscis – long mouthparts, like those on a butterfly.

Pupal – a stage in development of insects with incomplete metamorphosis, between the larva and adult. This is usually an immobile stage in which wings are visible but not functional.

Queen – the egg-laying member of a social insect colony.

Soldier – members of a social insect colony specialized for colony defense.

Species – the working unit of biodiversity, and the "kinds" of organisms we normally recognize as different (the House Fly, *Musca domestica*, is an example of a species).

Stigma – the part of the plant that receives pollen.

Vertebrates – organisms with a backbone and internal skeleton.

Workers – members of a social insect colony that do not lay eggs, and instead carry out other activities for the colony (such as gathering food).

DISCARDED

J 595.7 MARSHALL
Marshall, S. A.
Insects A to Z /
R0112678917   PTREE

PEACHTREE

Atlanta-Fulton Public Library